MW01610918

Printed in the United States of America

978-0-578-40535-3

Team Jamie Grace
9663 Santa Monica Blvd #962
Beverly Hills, California 90210

jamiegrace.com | @jamiegraceh

CONNECT WITH JAMIE GRACE

 @jamiegraceh on instagram, twitter + facebook

 subscribe to *The Jamie Grace Podcast* for daily podcast episodes on life, love, Faith, dating and relationships. available on Spotify, iTunes and all other free podcast apps

 second edition released in 2019: *boys, boys, boys: thoughts on dating* by jamie grace. available at Amazon.com suggested 13-18

 subscribe to *youtube.com/jgracepro* for weekly videos including music videos, acoustic songs and vlogs featuring jamie grace's husband aaron collins

 stream Jamie Grace's latest music on Apple Music, Spotify & more + visit jamiegrace.com for tour dates!

Made in the
USA
Monee, IL

This book is dedicated to my husband, aaron. As all married people [almost annoyingly] say, you were most definitely worth the wait.

- How To Use This Devotional -

- READ -

This is likely the most obvious choice. There are 15 devotionals that will each take less than 15 minutes to read. Some days may be good for now but better for later. Soak it in, be encouraged, and remember that you can always revisit any of the days or even read the devotional at a slower place if you need to.

- JOURNAL -

This devotional is designed to be able to be read and journaled-in more than once. Your choice to wait will have an incredible impact on your life and throughout different seasons in your journey, this devotional, **and *your* words**, will be a significant part of your story.

You will have seasons where waiting makes so much sense. You will have seasons where waiting is frustrating and you may doubt your choices. No one is perfect - not one - and there will be seasons where you will learn more about grace and mercy than you may have anticipated.

Every journal prompt has **four** different spaces, with dates included, to be journaled in during **four different seasons.** Write the date, and follow the prompt(s) to write the reality of where *your* heart is in that moment. In that season. When you revisit this devotional, do the same, and see how your heart, journey and story have changed and evolved over time.

Allow yourself to be as real and vulnerable as you can. This is *your* devotional. *Your* journal. Even if it's difficult or seemingly overwhelming at times, know that as you look back over how you've grown, you could have the potential to be encouraged, convicted or both. And trust me - they're both an equally beautiful part of growing, learning and becoming that absolute best version of yourself.

Wondering which season(s) in life should promote a visit back to this devotional? The best day for day 1 is always **right now**. Maybe your next day 1 could be during a season when...

- You start dating someone new
- You get engaged
- You're 15 days away from your wedding (***trust me***)
- A close friend or sibling gets engaged, married or in a new relationship
- You're going through a breakup
- Your birthday is coming up
- It's the start of a new year
- You're starting a new job or a new school
- It's Valentine's Day, Christmas or another Holiday

- MAKE STICKY NOTES -

Throughout this devotional, you'll come across scriptures, daily affirmations or quotes. Choose quotes and affirmations that **challenge** or encourage, and document them on your *Wait It Out* sticky notes. Post them on your bathroom mirror, nightstand, kitchen counter, bedroom ceiling or wherever you're mostly like to see them daily. If you'd like, you can share photos of your stick note(s) on social media, using the hashtags #WaitItOutDevotional and #WaitItOut.

- Introduction -

Too often the message of purity is said to exclusively mean to "save sex" for marriage. In high school I made the decision to "wait" for marriage and I'm *so* glad I did. Yet to glorify sex as the *only* thing worth waiting for is to diminish the true beauty of what love really is. To portray sex as the *only* thing worth waiting for gives us a false identity that sex is greater than any other element of a relationship; that it's worth sitting on a pedestal. In reality, it's one of many beautiful things designed to further build the connection between a man and wife.

I started my podcast *The Jamie Grace Podcast (formerly called Wait It Out)* to talk about life, love, dating, relationships and other things worth waiting for. My YouTube channel, songs, live shows *and* my podcast are all dedicated to sharing the message of purity in regards to our bodies, hearts *and* minds. In my early 20s I wrote a book called *Boys, Boys, Boys* all about dating, relationships and - boys, obviously and truly enjoyed sharing my thoughts, fears, hopes and dreams.

In my mid-20s, I started working on this book. I knew I wanted to write a devotional but also wanted to write something like a large compilation of sarcastic essays ranting about stuff that gets on my nerves. Sometimes I think my middle name was given to me out of the knowingness that I would need the reminder of what we all deserve...

Ultimately, I decided to do both. Both a devotional/workbook/journal type *and* a random rant collection about the things that stress me out a bit. If you're looking for the latter, so sorry but you picked up the wrong one.

However if you're single, dating someone or engaged and are waiting or considering waiting, I think you'll enjoy this book as well.

The next 15 days will be filled with devotionals, journal prompts, and encouragement as we journey through **waiting.**

Your heart.
Your mind.
Your body.
Your time.

These are all truly beautiful things that deserve to treated with the utmost respect. Not just your body. Not just your mind. Every single part of you is worth waiting for. I promise.

Whether you grew up knowing you wanted to "wait," whether you're just now considering it or whether you're reading this because your phone died and you're on an airplane and this is all that was in your bag and the airline's magazine just ain't cuttin' it, I hope this book reaches your heart. Truly.

- JOURNAL -

INTRODUCTION, SEASON #1:

DATE: _12_ / _26_ / _2020_

WHAT SEASON IN YOUR LIFE MADE YOU WANT TO READ THIS
DEVOTIONAL? The Lord just recently told me
who my future husband is! 💗💗💗

WHAT DOES "WAITING" MEAN TO YOU? Waiting to me
means not doing things I would
regret later that doesn't just mean
having sex. Things that I want to be
special only for my husband in general.

ARE YOU WAITING? WHY / WHY NOT? Yes. Partially
because of my beliefs but also
because I want the things I
do in marriage to only be in marriage
to make it that much more special.

(IF YES) WHAT HAS BEEN THE MOST CHALLENGING PART ABOUT
WAITING SO FAR? To be honest, I haven't
really had challenges with waiting
at this point of the wild journey
the Lord is taking me on.

Introduction, Season #2:

Date: _____ / _____ / _____

What season in your life prompted you want to read this devotional? _____
_____

What does "Waiting" mean to you? _____
_____
_____
_____

Are you waiting? Why / Why not? _____
_____
_____
_____

(if yes) What has been the most challenging part about waiting so far? _____
_____
_____
_____

INTRODUCTION, SEASON #3:

DATE: _____ / _____ / _____

WHAT SEASON IN YOUR LIFE PROMPTED YOU WANT TO READ THIS
DEVOTIONAL? _____
_____

WHAT DOES "WAITING" MEAN TO YOU? _____
_____
_____
_____

ARE YOU WAITING? WHY / WHY NOT? _____
_____
_____
_____

(IF YES) WHAT HAS BEEN THE MOST CHALLENGING PART ABOUT
WAITING SO FAR? _____
_____
_____
_____

INTRODUCTION, SEASON #4:

DATE: _____ / _____ / _____

WHAT SEASON IN YOUR LIFE PROMPTED YOU WANT TO READ THIS DEVOTIONAL? _____

_____

WHAT DOES "WAITING" MEAN TO YOU? _____

_____

_____

_____

ARE YOU WAITING? WHY / WHY NOT? _____

_____

_____

_____

(IF YES) WHAT HAS BEEN THE MOST CHALLENGING PART ABOUT WAITING SO FAR? _____

_____

_____

_____

- Day 1 -

It's likely that in this exact moment, you're single. And if you're single, then you have experienced the extremes. You have moments where a majority of people in your community push the extreme of getting married to find happiness. Often saying things like:

When will you settle down?
Why couldn't you have made it work with the last guy?
You're too picky.

Then there's the extreme on the other end of the spectrum, telling you that you'll only find love when you block out the world and live in the joy of *me, myself and I.* Some of their famous quotes are:

It'll happen when you least expect it.
I didn't meet my husband until I was 83 years old - just wait.
You're too young to be thinking about that, just enjoy your life right now.

During my years of singlehood, I constantly wanted to push the focus to the center: to find the beauty in desiring companionship while simultaneously celebrating a season of singlehood. I never stopped praying for my husband, yet I never stopped loving myself.

This balance is beautiful. Possible. Incredible. Sometimes difficult. Often frustrating. Not popular. But the balance is beautiful.

I wrote the following in September 2015. A little more than a year before I met my now husband Aaron. My life with Aaron is my absolute favorite and I'm so glad he showed up and we got married, etc etc etc this book isn't about our story. It's a journal for *your* journey and I want to share a rant I wrote in 2015 to accompany you in the waiting.

I was sitting on an airplane, anxious to write about being single and confident. Praying for my husband, while still absolutely proud of myself.

Here's what I came up with:

I'm rich. No, seriously. I have a signifiant amount of independent wealth.

Mostly on Mondays.

My Mondays are the days where my independent wealth primarily abounds.

And by *My Mondays* or a *Musician's Weekend,* I fully comprehend that that is potentially *Your Saturday.*

On Mondays I wake up around 11am. Sometimes even closer to 2pm, but mostly 11am. I roll out of my bed and go to the bathroom. Then I shower... maybe. I brush my teeth (this is not a maybe), handle some other essential business and get back in my bed. By Noon I've probably microwaved something random that looks pre-expired and I eat it. At this point I've probably turned on Hulu or Netflix and by 3pm, after my nap, I may run to the store.
I typically begin my Monday (your Saturday)'s productivity around 3pm and it most always starts with the grocery store.

I love the grocery store.

I spend at least an hour in there. I go through everything I want versus need, and spend forever debating on new recipes. I walk around at *least* 12 thousand times trying desperately to avoid the employees. I know they mean well, but I have my shopping experience down to an obsessive compulsive system. My OCD tendencies and my inability to lie to strangers make communicating with grocery store employees very difficult.

Once they see me wandering for a good half hour they ask, "Can I help you with something?" and I get stressed out. The truthful answer is "Yes, you *can.*" But the reality is that I don't *want* help. So what do I say: "No thank you"? That's what a normal human would say. But not me. I feel like I'm lying if I say "No." My gut wants to reply with, "Yes but I prefer to be independent." However I'm pretty sure that would put me on some sort of psycho-shopper list. I usually just say, "I'm good, thanks" and follow it up with a smile. A smile fixes everything... #lies.

I get my groceries, including my essentials (kale, chicken and cheese) for the weekend (a musician's weekend is a human's work week... there's no way you've not gotten that yet), maybe stop by a department store and get a new CD (I'm 90), possibly a shirt if it's cute and I return to my house.

Unless... there's a new movie out. Or a puppy adoption. Or a random art festival. Or if one of the girls I mentor calls and needs a post-mid-term-big-sis-hug. Or if a church kiddo has a soccer game or needs a FaceTime conversation. I don't really have a planned routine. There are things on my checklist that I need to do, that I definitely will do, but Monday is one of my few non-travel days of the week. Though I have work (emails, planning or filming videos, writing songs, etc) to do, it's the closest I have to an "off" day.

After I get home, it's usually pretty late. Late meaning early! That was lame. It's usually close to 9 or 10pm when I pull in my garage and I start cooking. That's right - cooking at 10pm. I like to cook at night because it's quiet. There's something about the peace that comes over my beating heart after the sun is down and it's windy outside. (When my dog lived with me this was my favorite time to take her for walks but apparently that's not safe).

Just before I start to cook I put a Donna Summers or Dolly Parton vinyl on one of my record players and Pinterest-recipe the night away. More often than not I fall asleep between 2-4am (just check my Twitter) and I wake up on Tuesday, my second and last "off day," and pretty much do the same thing over again.

Throughout both days I'm likely to have meetings, studio sessions, interviews, emails and other things as a part of the "upkeep" of my job but for the most part: **I am rich.**

I am constantly floating in an abundance of independent wealth. My parents, my covering, are great mentors but at 24, I'm definitely an adult. I make my own decisions regarding my finances, my sleep schedule, my Hulu, Netflix, etc. subscriptions, my eating habits, relationships, friendships, church involvement, the car that I drive, the events I attend and even the decision to purchase a new laptop cord. No one questions me, no one helps me budgets my money or time. It's me, myself and I. Sun up. Sun down. *Rich.*

Psst. If it's not obvious, when saying "rich," we're not talking about money.

Now, I don't want to come across as though I am bragging or trying to make anyone feel less than if they are not independently wealthy. No one (in this case I'm really just referring to myself) ever said anything about loving being rich or swimming excessively in my assets. My wealth and I have a pretty secure relationship but we hit instability on the occasional Sunday morning... and just about every Christmas... most Holidays, actually...

It's not always easy being "the single one." (And other things Captain Obvious would name his blog...) I've been on less than 10 first dates since I was 18 (less than 0 before then) and 2 second dates. For various reasons I can truly look back and know that I wasn't supposed to enter into a relationship with any of those guys but there are the moments where I wonder if my independence is all that great. Again, I have incredible parents, who are not only my parents and mentors but my pastors. My friends? Though a small circle, they're all I need. But how much independence is good for a soul not meant to be alone?

These are the thoughts that keep me up at night. Once I've made casseroles, turned on the crockpot and crawled into bed at 2am. These are the thoughts that keep me tossing at turning for another hour or two. I try to shut them off by turning on a movie or using social media but I can't help but realize how quiet my room is because I'm by myself. It's not even an anxiety geared from sexual desire but merely the fact of not wanting to be alone. Whoever thought it was fun to be rich... was wrong.

But then I wake up.

I wake up at my odd hour and go about my day without a care in the world and am overly excited to be wealthy in independence.

Certainly I'm not the only single person that has ever floated between gratitude and loneliness all in a 24 hour period. If it's not you, put this book away. I feel you judging me! Rude.

But, if it is you? What do you do? Or, better yet: what do *we* do? How do we balance this excitement of where our lives are in the now, while hoping for a future that grants us a best friend that's stuck with us forever because of love and law (#winning)?

We dance.

We dance in our wealth.

We do not boast on our gifts or our blessings but we dance in them for as long as they are there.

The ability to be a mentor young girls or guys in every ounce of our spare time.

Hopping on a plane to visit our friends or distant relatives and only having to pay for one ticket.

Cooking dinner for two, eating for one, and instantly having lunch for the next day.

Sleeping in or staying up late knowing that you're only messing up your own sleep schedule.

Buying those new shoes or whatever makes ya smile just because! (Don't overdo this one...)

Hanging out at a friend's house and crashing on their couch.

Giving college classes or career goals *all* of your time.

Cheaper eat-out nights.

Cheaper movie nights.

Cheaper **everything.**

Going a mission's trip or friend get-a-way weekend for multiple nights and not missing your spouse.

Traveling, late nights with friends, inconsistent sleep scheduling, random shopping, mentoring... these are all things that can happen while you're married. My sister, Morgan, has been married for five years and she and I have done all of those things together since she tied the knot. But we *certainly* did them together much more often when she was single.

Morgan has an amazing husband that she loves dearly and I love seeing how well they work together. I pray that someday she can say the same about me and my guy, but for now, I *have* to dance in the things that make make singlehood a beautiful place to be.

My husband is gonna be awesome. He's gonna be so much fun. And hopefully kind of loud and crazy at times. But right now... Jamie Grace is enough. I choose to accept that I am enough. I may be "alone" but it doesn't have to turn into loneliness. I'm too wealthy for that.

There is a significant amount of independent wealth in your season of singleness. Someday, you may be married, and **trust me** - there's a whole new vault that's been collecting interest with a percentage greater than you can imagine. But please, don't overlook the beauty in this very moment.

You are enough.
You are enough.
Pray for tomorrow. Hope for what it holds.
Dance today.
You are enough.
You are enough.

JOURNAL:

MAKE A LIST OF 10 THINGS THAT MAKE YOU INDEPENDENTLY
WEALTHY. LIST 20 THINGS THAT BRING OUT THE BEAUTY IN LIFE
YOU LIVE IN THIS PRESENT MOMENT.

DAY 1, SEASON #1:

DATE: _____ / _____ / _____

1. _____

2. _____

3. _____

4. _____

5. _____

6. _____

7. _____

8. _____

9. _____

10. _____

Day 1, Season #2:

Date: _____ / _____ / _____

1. _____
2. _____
3. _____
4. _____
5. _____
6. _____
7. _____
8. _____
9. _____
10. _____

Day 1, Season #3:

Date: _____ / _____ / _____

1. _____
2. _____
3. _____
4. _____
5. _____
6. _____

7. _____

8. _____

9. _____

10. _____

DAY 1, SEASON #4:

DATE: _____ / _____ / _____

1. _____

2. _____

3. _____

4. _____

5. _____

6. _____

7. _____

8. _____

9. _____

10. _____

- DAY 2 -

He doesn't like you...

    I remember the first time I said these words to myself. I was standing in the mirror, as dramatic humans do, with absolutely no facial expression. I took a deep breath, made direct eye contact with my reflection and said, "He doesn't like you..." After I said, I stood in those words that were floating around me. I let them sink.
    Then, I finished the sentence.
    "He doesn't like you... and that's okay."

Simple.
Sweet.
Awkward.
Realistic.
Painful.
Necessary.

    I've had moments where I've been convinced that I could be a professional drama queen. I could probably pick up a paycheck or two from some office hiring over-thinkers who beat themselves up unnecessarily. But in this moment, I wasn't overreacting. I wasn't being too dramatic. I was allowing myself to face the reality of a situation that wasn't going to change.
    Whether it's a romantic interest that isn't mutual or a friendship that isn't going to happen, it's so easy to over analyze every moment, anticipating for a magical change when we often know the truth. *She doesn't want to hang out with you* or *He's not interested in you*. These aren't depressing sentences or heart wrenching facts - **this is the first step into your freedom.**

I don't want to diminish the heartache that often comes after a breakup or when a friendship falls a part. I understand the pain and the tears and insecurity that show up when you like someone and it isn't mutual or you've tried everything you can to "treat others the way you want to be treated" and every door keeps slamming in your face. This pain is real. These things take time to recover from, and you shouldn't feel guilty about going that grieving process.

Through it all, I want to help you find your freedom.
I want to help you rediscover your worth.
I want to help you step into an understanding of where your worth and value come from.
I want to help you find and trust the source of your strength so that nothing can come eradicate the strong person you are.

Is there someone that you like right now? Is there someone that you're interested in but it's not mutual? Did you recently go through a break up?

I want you to do something that might feel incredibly awkward. But the good news is, no one will see you, so you'll be alright. Go to your bathroom, stand in front your mirror, and look into your eyes and say it. This isn't a long speech about every sad memory since 2nd grade, but simply a sentence. Or maybe two. You can use your own words, or start with one of these:

I'm single.
He doesn't like me.
We broke up.
He's dating someone else.
We're not together anymore.
He stopped texting.

He didn't call.
I don't know where we stand.

Then, take a deep breath. **Smile.** Put your shoulders back. Relax your hands (just incase they randomly made a fist). Lift your chin up. Breathe. Smile. Say, **"And I am okay."** Say until you believe it. Say it every day. Write it down. Sing it. Scream it. Cry it. Believe it.

Your world isn't over. Your value hasn't changed. Your worth hasn't diminished. Your beauty hasn't gone away. Your character doesn't have to suffer. You are still the **same** incredible person that you were **before all of this!** Own it. Live it.

Journal:

Day 2, Season #1:

Date: 12 / 27 / 2020

WHAT IS SOMETHING THAT YOU'RE LEARNING TO ACCEPT, THAT IS A PART OF STEPPING INTO **YOUR** FREEDOM? I am "who the Lord made me to be in every way, shape and form. He loves me as I am, not as the person I want to be that I'm not.

Day 2, Season #2:

Date: _____ / _____ / _____

WHAT IS SOMETHING THAT YOU'RE LEARNING TO ACCEPT, THAT IS A PART OF STEPPING INTO **YOUR** FREEDOM? _____

_____

_____

_____

DAY 2, SEASON #3:

DATE: _____ / _____ / _____

WHAT IS SOMETHING THAT YOU'RE LEARNING TO ACCEPT, THAT
IS A PART OF STEPPING INTO **YOUR** FREEDOM? _____

_____

_____

_____

DAY 2, SEASON #4:

DATE: _____ / _____ / _____

WHAT IS SOMETHING THAT YOU'RE LEARNING TO ACCEPT, THAT
IS A PART OF STEPPING INTO **YOUR** FREEDOM? _____

_____

_____

_____

- DAY 3 -

*if he doesn't like you, that doesn't mean
there's anything wrong with you.*

*if he doesn't like you, that doesn't mean
there's anything wrong with him.*

*it might just mean that you're two humans
who simply aren't meant to be. your worth
doesn't change. your value hasn't
decreased.* **@JAMIEGRACEH**

- DAY 4 -

I like food. Yes, I like healthy stuff, it's a good idea to exercise, moderation is key, etc. This isn't a book about health or nutrition so we're going to talk about one of my best friends: pizza.

I don't want to offend anyone from Chicago. Or New York. There are so many different kinds of pizza and some truly authentic styles. Please consider this my disclaimer to save myself from tweets saying I explained the magic of pizza wrong. I just want to talk about cheese, y'all. Just let me talk about cheese.

If we're talking food-related happiness, cheesy pizza is the source. One of my favorite restaurants up North takes about an hour to make a pizza. You're sitting there anticipating the best pizza of your entire life and when it shows up, it's definitely worth the wait.

I love the stuffed pizza. It's a layer of dough, a ton of toppings, an excessive amount of cheese, and another layer of dough on top. THEN they add the sauce. After what feels like 6 months of waiting for it, they bring the source of my happiness to the table and I don't talk to anyone for a solid 24 hours (I don't talk while I'm eating, then I fall sleep, then I wake up and eat whatever's left).

I like to eat their stuffed pizza with sausage and cheese. Keep it simple. It smells good, tastes better, and because I love it so much, it's almost as if nothing can stand in my way.

I'm very passionate about food. And as much as I love cheese, I have the same amount of hate for other toppings. For example: mushrooms. I don't understand how anyone could eat such a small, odd, rubbery, funny shaped thing. It genuinely upsets me when a restaurant tells me that they're cooked into the meal I want, because I won't *knowingly* order or eat a mushroom. They hurt my feelings. I don't like them. At all. At all. At all.

A few years ago, I was up North and was sitting down to enjoy this amazing pizza restaurant that I love. It took forever to order, and even longer for the food to arrive at our table. But as this particular sausage and cheese **(only)** pizza is the source of my food-related happiness, I was already in a great mood, knowing that I would soon be connected to the source.

It arrived. I was beaming. I try to be a kind and dignified human but when it comes to pizza I'm not ashamed to make my plate first and dig in. (We prayed earlier because we had appetizers I just don't need anyone getting distracted from the point of this story okay back to my meal). So I did. It was incredible. Truly, phenomenal.

Until…

The moment…

It was rubbery…

And weird…

I'm literally frowning just thinking about it…

Weirdly shaped…

The worst flavor… (also known as no flavor)

Y'all, it was a mushroom.

I was pretty upset. I'm not sure who I was mad at or how I got so angry so fast about the tiniest "problem" but I wasn't happy. I was annoyed. I was grossed out. I inspected the rest of my pizza. I didn't find anymore mushrooms. But I also wasn't positive because I didn't want to demolish a beautiful stuffed pizza looking for something so small.

I checked with the waiter. He confirmed that my order was placed correctly, and it was likely a mistake made in the kitchen. He offered to have it remade. I debated, with myself, if I should send it back and wait another hour to get another pizza. Or if I should just wing it.

Ultimately, I decided I would just get over it. Don't get me wrong - mushrooms are not for my life. I'm not into them. At all. But I love pizza so much. I had been anticipating this time with this pizza. I waited and waited. It showed up, and it brought me *so* much joy.

Would I allow one, small, tiny, flavor-less mistake to ruin an entirely wonderful experience? Mushrooms aren't bad for everyone. I just don't like them. At all. I gave them a chance once, it just didn't work for me. And in this moment, it surprised me completely and was a major disappointment. But when I compared the frustration of a mushroom to the joy of the pizza... the mushroom didn't matter that much at all.

The risk of finding another one while eating almost seemed... worth it. I was so connected to my food-related source of happiness, that I wasn't afraid of a mistake along the way. An awkward moment. Because I knew the source would be there no matter what.

When you are connected to a strong and solid source, there is no mistake or downfall that can overtake the joy that the source is providing.

You may fall sometimes. Well, you're human. You *will* fall sometimes. You'll feel defeated. Distraught. Discouraged. You will make mistakes. Someone else will make a mistake. You will disappoint someone. They will disappoint you.

You may be interested in someone that doesn't like you back. You may go through a breakup. You may break up with someone or they may break with up you. You might think you're dating someone while their worldview is a glorified friendship.

Make sure you're connected to a source.

Make sure you're connected to a well that never runs dry. A peace that passes all understanding. A joy that can't be taken away. A source that provides a hope for your future whether you have plans or not. A love greater than what anyone on Earth could even attempt to give you. Make sure you're connected to **The** source.

That mushroom was a mistake. And while you may love mushrooms (praying for you), we're all able to recognize that life is full of mistakes. Whether our own or someone else's, our broken world will continue to be a source of hurt feelings, awkward conversations and broken hearts. The question is - what is the source that you're leaning on? Depending on? Where do you go for your hope and joy?

When you're connected to a source that will never let you down, there is no mistake that could tear you a part. You may be filled with absolute fear, frustration and maybe even anger, but it will be no match to the polar opposites the source provides.

People often ask me why I seem to be smiling all of the time. I have faced a significant amount of adversity in my life and have had many moments where I felt like it was easier to just give up. I was bullied most of my life, have faced depression on and off, dealt with being mistreated by mentors that I trusted and have battled the daily struggles of Tourette Syndrome, OCD, ADHD and Anxiety since I was in middle school. Yet, real talk, I smile a lot.

I also cry a lot. If we're being real. I allow pain to be a thing and don't overlook my insecurities and frustrations. But my sorrow doesn't last forever. My heartache doesn't become the most prominent part of my existence. My disappointment in myself, or others, may seem like a dark cloud but a storm has to end at some point.

I remember spending a Summer getting to know a guy, for him to tell me that he saw me as a sister in Christ and nothing more. *After* I had introduced him to all of my family and friends.

I remember telling a guy, to his face, that I liked him. Only for him to immediately say he hoped I hadn't been anticipated being in a relationship. *After* our families spent a weekend together. He drove me back to the home where I was staying and went into another room with his brother and cried. That was great.

I remember being kissed in my early 20s. I didn't want him to do it. I was saving that for my husband. I asked him not to do it, but he did it anyway. I cried so much that night. The night he took that from me. The night that took me years to tell my counselor. My parents. The night that I wept telling my fiancé (now husband) about. The night that something was stolen from me.

I have experienced adversity.

I have experienced pain.

I have experienced miserable and overwhelming situations.

I have cried.

I have screamed.

I have prayed.

I have spent so much on counseling, y'all.

But The Source...

The Source where I find my strength...

The Source where I find my hope...

The Source doesn't prove that there will never be heartache or pain.

But The Source proves that it will always be **greater.**

I LIFT UP MY EYES TO THE MOUNTAINS—
WHERE DOES MY HELP COME FROM?
MY HELP COMES FROM THE LORD,
THE MAKER OF HEAVEN AND EARTH.
HE WILL NOT LET YOUR FOOT SLIP—
HE WHO WATCHES OVER YOU WILL NOT SLUMBER;
INDEED, HE WHO WATCHES OVER ISRAEL
WILL NEITHER SLUMBER NOR SLEEP.
THE LORD WATCHES OVER YOU—
THE LORD IS YOUR SHADE AT YOUR RIGHT HAND;
THE SUN WILL NOT HARM YOU BY DAY,
NOR THE MOON BY NIGHT.
THE LORD WILL KEEP YOU FROM ALL HARM—
HE WILL WATCH OVER YOUR LIFE;
THE LORD WILL WATCH OVER YOUR COMING AND GOING
BOTH NOW AND FOREVERMORE.

-PSALM 121

JOURNAL:

DATE: _____ / _____ / _____

CUSTOMIZE PSALM 121 TO ACCEPT THE INCREDIBLE REALITY OF
WHO **THE SOURCE** IS TO YOU. SOME BLANKS WILL BE YOUR
NAME, SOME WILL BE HIM/HER.

_____ LIFTS UP _____ EYES TO THE MOUNTAINS—
WHERE DOES _____ HELP COME FROM?
_____ HELP COMES FROM THE LORD,
THE MAKER OF HEAVEN AND EARTH.
HE WILL NOT LET _____ FOOT SLIP—
HE WHO WATCHES OVER _____ WILL NOT SLUMBER;
INDEED, HE WHO WATCHES OVER ISRAEL
WILL NEITHER SLUMBER NOR SLEEP.
THE LORD WATCHES OVER _____—
THE LORD IS _____'S SHADE AT _____'S RIGHT
HAND;
THE SUN WILL NOT HARM _____ BY DAY,
NOR THE MOON BY NIGHT.
THE LORD WILL KEEP _____ FROM ALL HARM—
HE WILL WATCH OVER _____'S LIFE;
THE LORD WILL WATCH OVER _____'S COMING AND
GOING
BOTH NOW AND FOREVERMORE.

- DAY 5 -

I was picking up dinner for my parents at a local restaurant about two years ago and struck up a conversation with a guy and his girl while we were all waiting for our food. After we exchanged the hi-how-are-you-me-too-how's-the-weather small talk, he told me that something really good must've just happened in my life because I was in a really good mood. I told him that I was ironically grabbing food to take to the hospital as my mom had been admitted about a week before.

He told me that it didn't make any sense. He wasn't being rude. He was simply asking how I seemed cheerful and excited when my story was clearly the opposite.

Oh is she about to come home from the hospital?
No.
Well, is she getting better?
Not really.
What's wrong?
She has a rare condition that doctors don't really understand.

...Then how in the world are you still smiling?

In that moment, I had the incredible privilege of telling him about the Source. The Source of my hope, joy, peace, strength and refuge. I told him about the love of Jesus. About the grace of God. About a peace that passes all understanding when all I *want* is understanding and could pass on the peace.

He had heard it before but didn't shut it down. He preferred a debate. More questioning. He wanted to know how I could consider myself lucky enough to have that kind of access. "What makes *us* so good that God would do all of that for us?" I can still hear the brokenness in his question. The desperation to cling to something greater than himself but the fear that he wasn't enough to receive that kind of love.

Before we can truly live in the joy that this life brings... the joys of singlehood, friendships, family, marriage, children, the list you made on day 1... we have to understand the Source of where all things beautiful come from.

We have to understand and accept the Source of our joy and our strength. The Source that validates who we are and who we were created to be.

The Source is the King of all kings.
The Source is the Lord of all lords.
The Source is the Creator above all creators.

THE LORD IS MY SHEPHERD; I SHALL NOT WANT...
-PSALM 23:1

YOU OPEN YOUR HAND;
YOU SATISFY THE DESIRE OF EVERY LIVING THING.
THE LORD IS RIGHTEOUS IN ALL HIS WAYS
AND KIND IN ALL HIS WORKS.
-PSALM 145:16

When we are able to acknowledge that **God is the source of everything we will *ever* need,** we are able to celebrate life in a new way. We are able to have joy in the midst of what may be the greatest pain. We are able to have hope in moments of absolute despair. We are able to find peace during all chaos.

When we accept that God is the source of everything we need, we embrace all that He has given us. We celebrate the breath in our lungs and people in our lives. The jobs we have because we were blessed with the talents and skills to not only apply but to get accepted and serve well. The churches we attend as a result of incredible people building incredible community.

And yes. We celebrate singlehood.

If we believe that it's all God… if we believe that He has His hand in every moment… if we believe that He is the reason for all that we have then we believe that the season that we are in is because of Him. Singlehood included. We aren't waiting for a **reward** of marriage, because the reward is *life - no matter what season.*

When we proclaim that God is the source of everything we need, we are able to truly celebrate independent wealth as a beautiful thing and a season of singlehood as a reason to rejoice.

Journal:

Day 5, Season #1:

Date: _____ / _____ / _____

WHAT ARE SOME CHALLENGES IN YOUR LIFE THAT YOU HAVE
FACED OR ARE FACING? WHAT ARE SOME THINGS YOU WISH YOU
COULD CHANGE? _____
_____
_____
_____

HOW HAS YOUR FAITH CARRIED YOU THROUGH THOSE MOMENTS?
_____
_____
_____
_____

WHAT ARE WAYS YOU COULD DEPEND ON GOD IN THE MIDST OF
THE CHALLENGES YOU MAY HAVE FACED/BE FACING?
_____
_____
_____
_____

Day 5, Season #2:

Date: _____ / _____ / _____

What are some challenges in your life that you have faced or are facing? What are some things you wish you could change? _____

_____

_____

_____

How has your Faith carried you through those moments?

_____

_____

_____

_____

What are ways you could depend on God in the midst of the challenges you may have faced/be facing?

_____

_____

_____

_____

DAY 5, SEASON #3:

DATE: _____ / _____ / _____

WHAT ARE SOME CHALLENGES IN YOUR LIFE THAT YOU HAVE
FACED OR ARE FACING? WHAT ARE SOME THINGS YOU WISH YOU
COULD CHANGE? _____
_____
_____
_____

HOW HAS YOUR FAITH CARRIED YOU THROUGH THOSE MOMENTS?
_____
_____
_____
_____

WHAT ARE WAYS YOU COULD DEPEND ON GOD IN THE MIDST OF
THE CHALLENGES YOU MAY HAVE FACED/BE FACING?
_____
_____
_____
_____

Day 5, Season #4:

Date: _____ / _____ / _____

What are some challenges in your life that you have faced or are facing? What are some things you wish you could change? _____

_____

_____

_____

How has your Faith carried you through those moments?

_____

_____

_____

_____

What are ways you could depend on God in the midst of the challenges you may have faced/be facing?

_____

_____

_____

_____

- Day 6 -

When Adam and Eve were in the Garden of Eden, God gave them some pretty simple instructions. In reading through the book of Genesis you can get incredible insight to all of the beautiful things in the garden as well as a guideline to live by.

THE LORD GOD MADE ALL KINDS OF TREES GROW OUT OF THE GROUND—
TREES THAT WERE PLEASING TO THE EYE AND GOOD FOR FOOD. IN THE
MIDDLE OF THE GARDEN WERE THE TREE OF LIFE AND THE TREE OF THE
KNOWLEDGE OF GOOD AND EVIL.

A RIVER WATERING THE GARDEN FLOWED FROM EDEN; FROM THERE IT
WAS SEPARATED INTO FOUR HEADWATERS. THE NAME OF THE FIRST IS
THE PISHON; IT WINDS THROUGH THE ENTIRE LAND OF HAVILAH, WHERE
THERE IS GOLD. (THE GOLD OF THAT LAND IS GOOD; AROMATIC RESIN AND
ONYX ARE ALSO THERE.) THE NAME OF THE SECOND RIVER IS THE GIHON;
IT WINDS THROUGH THE ENTIRE LAND OF CUSH. THE NAME OF THE THIRD
RIVER IS THE TIGRIS; IT RUNS ALONG THE EAST SIDE OF ASHUR. AND THE
FOURTH RIVER IS THE EUPHRATES.

THE LORD GOD TOOK THE MAN AND PUT HIM IN THE GARDEN OF EDEN TO
WORK IT AND TAKE CARE OF IT. AND THE LORD GOD COMMANDED THE
MAN, "YOU ARE FREE TO EAT FROM ANY TREE IN THE GARDEN; BUT YOU
MUST NOT EAT FROM THE TREE OF THE KNOWLEDGE OF GOOD AND
EVIL, FOR WHEN YOU EAT FROM IT YOU WILL CERTAINLY DIE."

GENESIS 2:9-17

If we were to take the last few words from that passage, it would sound purely miserable. "For when you eat from it will certainly die" - what in the world?! Out of context, it could easily sound like an unrighteously angry and unjust controller. It could sound like there's irrational punishment, and no glimpse of a gift.

However, when we're provided with context - the entire text - we're able to see that it's reasonable to have guidelines, just as with any relationship. Whether it's wedding vows, the expectations a teacher shares with their classroom or a lecture from a parent to a child. Every relationship has (should have…) beautiful, exciting, amazing and wonderful things *and* it's likely that every relationship has guidelines as well.

God's love for Adam and Eve was apparent in many ways, with the beauty of the garden being one of them. The trees and the rivers are just some of the examples of that beauty. Then there's **freedom. Oh, the freedom.** *You are free to eat from any tree.* The garden of Eden wasn't a punishment. It was freedom. There was merely one thing that God told them not to do. But in the grand scheme of all of the things He said that they *could* do? (reminder: total freedom) The restriction shouldn't seem that bad.

The best part of it all, is that God even gives a *reason* as to why they should refrain from the tree of the knowledge of good and evil. We don't always know the answer to every "why" - and that's okay. Yet in this text, God says, "for when you eat from it you will certainly die." This isn't a *because I said so* situation. There's a reason to refrain, and the choice is ours.

Before we go into the potentially obvious analogies of waiting and purity, I want to skip ahead in this story a little bit. In the next chapter, Adam and Eve eat from the tree. I've had my share of moments where I'm like, "Really, y'all?! You had **complete freedom** and you broke the **one** rule?!" But let's be real - that's simply my pride. We've all had that *one* thing that we didn't *have* to do and we knew we weren't *supposed* to do it - but we did it anyway.

Immediately after Adam and Eve ate from the tree, they realized they were naked. Before eating from the tree their nakedness went unnoticed. There was no sense of shame or vulnerability or insecurity until this moment - when they sinned.

Moments later, they're interacting with God (This is such a paraphrase - you've *got* to read the full book of Genesis) and you would think that the first thing out of a sees-all knows-all ruler's mouth would be the apparent punishment he warned them about… but it isn't. **He extends grace.**

He asks them what happened. Giving them the chance to explain themselves, instead of immediately calling them out for their wrongdoing. They don't die right away. Real talk, they keep living. God chooses life over death. He chooses forgiveness over wrath.

Adam and Eve are still punished, for God is a just God. He has a righteous anger about Him and knows that we are capable of following His commandments, so there are still consequences for our actions. Adam and Eve were no longer allowed to be in the Garden of Eden, yet God made garments ("of skin" as the Bible says, i.e. He sacrificed an animal) for them, as their nakedness was now apparent.

Interrupting myself to encourage you to really dig in to Genesis chapters 1-3. There's some really, really good better-than-a-TV-drama business in there that absolutely shouldn't be missed.

Even when we straight up mess up, there is grace. When we make a mistake. When we make a poor choice. When someone tempts us. When we tempt someone else. We are given the opportunity to tell God what's up - to confess. And like any **good** parent, God is just, and there will be consequences. But like any **great** parent, there is grace. There is mercy. There is follow through *and* forgiveness.

Journal:

"...For all have sinned and fall short of the glory of God..." -Romans 3:23

Temptation is just as real in our lives as it was for Adam and Eve. But so is God's grace.

Day 6, Season #1:

Date: _____ / _____ / _____

Have you faced temptation while waiting? _____
_____
_____

Through it all, God's grace prevails. Take a moment to thank him for His grace that has never, and will never, let us down. _____
_____
_____

DAY 6, SEASON #2:

DATE: _____ / _____ / _____

HAVE YOU FACED TEMPTATION WHILE WAITING? _____
_____
_____

THROUGH IT ALL, GOD'S GRACE PREVAILS. TAKE A MOMENT TO
THANK HIM FOR HIS GRACE THAT HAS NEVER, AND WILL NEVER,
LET US DOWN. _____
_____
_____

DAY 6, SEASON #3:

DATE: _____ / _____ / _____

HAVE YOU FACED TEMPTATION WHILE WAITING? _____
_____
_____

THROUGH IT ALL, GOD'S GRACE PREVAILS. TAKE A MOMENT TO
THANK HIM FOR HIS GRACE THAT HAS NEVER, AND WILL NEVER,
LET US DOWN. _____
_____

Day 6, Season #4:

Date: _____ / _____ / _____

Have you faced temptation while waiting? _____
_____
_____

Through it all, God's grace prevails. Take a moment to thank him for His grace that has never, and will never, let us down. _____
_____
_____

- Day 7 -

*there is no more or less grace
for anyone based on their sexual
history.*

*plain and simple: sex isn't
greater than grace.*

@JAMIEGRACEH

- DAY 8 -

So now - we talk about sex.

When understanding the choice to wait for physical intimacy - without context - it could easily sound like the excessive and unnecessary rules of an unrighteously angry and unjust controller. It could sound like there are irrational expectations with no glimpse of a gift. "Hey you know what sex is right? Yeah don't have it 'cause you're a follower of Christ." - No. That's not how this works.

When we're provided with context, we're able to see that it's reasonable to have guidelines, just as with any relationship. Whether it's wedding vows, the expectations a teacher shares with their classroom or a lecture from a parent to a child. Every relationship has (should have...) beautiful, exciting, amazing and wonderful things *and* it's likely that every relationship has guidelines as well.

It would take the rest of this book to really break down *every* time the word of God talks about relationships, intimacy, love and sex. However, it's so apparent that God not only provides context for sex, but provides context for it to be a **beautiful** thing. And with that beauty, we see the guidelines as well.

THE HUSBAND SHOULD FULFILL HIS WIFE'S SEXUAL NEEDS, AND THE WIFE SHOULD FULFILL HER HUSBAND'S NEEDS. THE WIFE GIVES AUTHORITY OVER HER BODY TO HER HUSBAND, AND THE HUSBAND GIVES AUTHORITY OVER HIS BODY TO HIS WIFE.
1 CORINTHIANS 7:3-5

FOR THIS REASON A MAN WILL LEAVE HIS FATHER AND MOTHER AND BE UNITED TO HIS WIFE, AND THEY WILL BECOME ONE FLESH.
GENESIS 2:24

SONG OF SOLOMON 7:6
PROVERBS 5:18-19

JOURNAL:

DO YOU WANT TO WAIT? ARE YOU WAITING? ARE YOU
CONSIDERING WAITING? WHAT DOES IT MEAN TO WAIT? WHY ARE
YOU WAITING? WHY IS IT IMPORTANT TO YOU? WHAT ARE THE
BENEFITS OF WAITING? IS THERE ANY DIFFICULT ABOUT
WAITING? WILL IT BE WORTH IT TO WAIT? WHY?

DAY 8, SEASON #1:

DATE: _____ / _____ / _____

WHY IS WAITING IMPORTANT TO YOU? _____

_____

_____

_____

_____

WHAT HAVE YOU LEARNED WHILE WAITING? _____

_____

_____

_____

_____

DAY 8, SEASON #2:

DATE: _____ / _____ / _____

WHY IS WAITING IMPORTANT TO YOU? _____
_____
_____
_____
_____

WHAT HAVE YOU LEARNED WHILE WAITING? _____
_____
_____
_____
_____

DAY 8, SEASON #3:

DATE: _____ / _____ / _____

WHY IS WAITING IMPORTANT TO YOU? _____
_____
_____
_____
_____

WHAT HAVE YOU LEARNED WHILE WAITING? _____

_____

_____

_____

_____

DAY 8, SEASON #4:

DATE: _____ / _____ / _____

WHY IS WAITING IMPORTANT TO YOU? _____

_____

_____

_____

_____

WHAT HAVE YOU LEARNED WHILE WAITING? _____

_____

_____

_____

_____

- DAY 9 -

My favorite food is Cheeseburger Pie. It's something like a quiche meets macaroni & cheese after a house party with pizza. Which, we've established how much I love cheese... and pizza... so clearly this is something I am borderline obsessed with.

I tasted my mom's Cheeseburger Pie for the first time when I was about 7. She would make it in four little individual casserole dishes so that she, my dad, sister and I would all have our own little meals. Brilliant, that lady. Epitome of brilliant.

For my 16th birthday my mom came up with the idea of throwing *Jamie Grace's Sweet Sixteen: Her 16 Favorite Things.* I got to invite 16 friends and the party, a sleepover, lasted for 16 hours. Some of my favorite things included orange soda, directing music videos, playing worship music... we had it on a Saturday night and it ended the next morning at church where my friends were picked up. Great sleepover idea: my parent's didn't have to drive all over to Georgia to deliver my precious friends back to their respective homes. :-)

As you may have guessed, one of the things high on the list was cheeseburger pie. It's not the healthiest "pie" in the world so it's a rarity in our house but it was my birthday so we just *had* to. My mom started cooking it just before my friends came over and before I knew it the smell of my favorite meal was seeping throughout the entire house.

As the evening went on I found myself repeatedly ditching my friends from our music video set and joining my mom in the kitchen like the average kid on a long road trip. "Is it ready yet?" Ten minutes later. "How about now?" "Mom, I'm starving. This is what death feels like." An hour later. "Mom... mom... now?" (Note, this is not a dialogue. She didn't respond, just gave me the *look*. Serious enough for me to dip out but sweet enough for me to know I could come back later - follow through *and* forgiveness.)

As we got closer to actually eating, I asked again, and this time I actually got a response. As I, naturally, think of my life as a playwright and/or musical (depending on the scene and characters, of course), the conversation went a little something like this:

Me: Hey mom, is it ready yet?

Mom: No Jamie, I'll let you know when it is.

Me: Well, can I just taste it?

Mom: No, Jamie, it's not ready.

Me: Well like, what if I just tasted a little?

Mom: You'd probably get sick.

Me: What do you mean? No I wouldn't.

Mom: Yes you would. I know what I'm talking about. There's raw food in it that has too cook.

Me: Yeah I know but like it looks ready, like, the cheese is melted and I know you say it's not ready but I'm pretty sure it is. If you would just let me taste it...

Mom: Just because it looks and smells ready, doesn't mean that it is. You have to trust me, I'm the one cooking it, you're just waiting to eat it. If you eat it now it might taste good for a minute, but after it settles you'll get sick and start blaming everyone else for not stopping you... you'll eventually blame yourself and while you'll feel better later, it's going

```
to take a while and it might take even longer to even
want to eat cheeseburger pie again. Go hang out with
your friends. I'll let you know when it's ready. Trust
me.
```

I didn't realize until years later that that would become one of my favorite moments with my mom. When I look back and see my antsy self dancing around the kitchen and my patient mom working hard I don't think either one of us knew the metaphor that was being developed in this sweet, tender, cheesy moment.

Have you ever wanted something so badly but it just wasn't ready yet? Your favorite meal, a package in the mail, your birthday... a date with the hott guy you see everyday but you're positive he's never seen you?

If we chase relationships... if we become anxious about sex... if we are too eager to be physically and emotionally intimate, we could end up miserable. In the moment it may feel good, *really* good, but when its over we'll realize the long term affect that it has.

It's kind of like eating food before it's ready. We hear the person cooking it tell us time and time again that we need to be patient... not snacking on little parts as we go and trying to find a way out of being still. But instead, we should wait until the creator has completely finished the meal they've prepared so we can sit and enjoy it at once.

God, the creator, wants us to wait. God wants us to exercise patience. God wants us to enjoy sex, not resent it. To celebrate sex, not run away from it. He gives us a beautiful gift and all He asks is that we accept the guidelines He has laid out for us.

Waiting to have sex isn't a punishment. Instead, it's a chance to enjoy sex in total freedom. It's enjoying something in the context that it was intended to be enjoyed in, so that it can be enjoyed in total **freedom.**

Journal:

Day 8, Season #1:

Date: _____ / _____ / _____

Do you find it easy to trust God while you're waiting?
Why/why not? _____

_____

_____

_____

_____

_____

Day 8, Season #2:

Date: _____ / _____ / _____

Do you find it easy to trust God while you're waiting?
Why/why not? _____

_____

_____

_____

_____

_____

Day 8, Season #3:

Date: _____ / _____ / _____

Do you find it easy to trust God while you're waiting? Why/why not? _____

_____

_____

_____

_____

_____

Day 8, Season #4:

Date: _____ / _____ / _____

Do you find it easy to trust God while you're waiting? Why/why not? _____

_____

_____

_____

_____

_____

- DAY 10 -

I remember making the choice to wait. While my Faith played a significant part in making that decision, there were other elements as well. I wanted to make sure that my health was a priority. I didn't want to be emotionally attached to someone without know what our future was and the idea of saying things like "pregnancy scare" seemed overwhelming to me.

Now that I'm married, I can truly say that it was worth the wait. When I was single, I felt like married people were always saying that, but even through the frustration and temptation that I faced, I always hoped I would understand that phrase someday.

Whether you have been waiting or you're at the start of your journey, it can still be worth the wait. *The Wait* is no more or less beautiful based on having waited since 7th grade verses waiting since 7am this morning. The wait *will* be worth it, and here are a few reasons why.

1) THERE ARE NO QUESTIONS, FEARS OR WORRIES ABOUT "SAFE SEX" OR SEXUAL HISTORY.

When you're not sexually active, you are eradicating any worry or fear of packing protection, risking your health or any similar concern. If you're planning on getting married, these are *valid* conversations to have with your future spouse - before you say *I do*. But imagine only having these conversations with *one* person instead of over and over again.

2) THERE IS NO COMPARISON.

To some people, this would be a disadvantage to waiting. Questions like, "How will you know what you like?" Or "How do you know it couldn't be better than what it is?" may show up. As someone who was pretty inexperienced pre-marriage, I'm *glad* I don't have any other experiences to compare my husband to. Our bodies were made for this stuff, yo. You're not inventing a new physical activity. Trust me, your stuff knows where it goes. With healthy communication before and during marriage, and just straight up taking time to be married - you figure it out.

Waiting to have sex is **not** choosing to be silent about sex and the reality of desiring it. For most people, the wedding night sex won't be the same as sex on your 5 to 10 year wedding anniversary. But when you have your entire lives to enjoy each other, you're able to appreciate that your spouse is *the* person that you're enjoying.

3) THERE IS NO NEED TO EMOTIONALLY DISENGAGE WITH SOMEONE WHO DIDN'T PROMISE FOREVER.

When you have sex, there is both a physical and emotional connection. It's my opinion and it's also science. When you choose to have sex after the commitment of forever has been made, you know that every experience is a part of bringing you all closer to each other. Without that commitment, you're left with the need to detach yourself from the very thing that was used to develop an attachment.

If you have formed that physical and/or emotional connection with someone and you want to start waiting and working toward no longer having that connection, **you can do that.** You're not broken, ruined or demolished. Your story is simply your story. Your past is your past. It's your choice, right now, how you live out your future.

4) THERE IS NO WORRY OF THE FUTURE.

Marriage isn't a trap to say, "I got one! He can never leave!" And we also don't know exactly what anyone's future holds (Proverbs 27:1), including our own. However, marriage is a beautiful commitment of your vows to love and cherish each other forever.

When you have made this commitment, intimacy is freeing. You're allowed to drop all insecurities of vulnerability, awkwardness, wonderfulness and newness. You can be unapologetically *you* without worrying if he'll leave in the morning, if he's ready for a long term commitment or if he'll leave once he finds out *everything* about you.

When he's your husband, he'll be there in the morning.

When he's your husband, he has publicly committed to the long term.

When he's your husband, he already knows everything. The good, bad and the hot mess, yet he **chooses** you.

That's marriage, y'all. It's not bondage. It's not a restriction. It's choosing someone daily. Choosing everything about them to celebrate and embrace, on the days where that comes easy and the days where it's - you guessed it - a choice. It's such an exceptionally freeing union.

When we put sex on an unnecessary pedestal, we either obsess over how much sex we *should* have or decide that it's our main goal in life to punish anyone who isn't doing it right. Sex is a beautiful, contextual thing. We've established that. But know that it's merely a *part* of marriage.

Sex isn't marriage and marriage isn't sex. Sex is a part of becoming, and staying of, one flesh. But I would also add that so is communication and so are date nights. Road trips and TV marathons. Cuddling, kissing, planning for the future and so much more.

When we look at all of the exceptional gifts we've been given, we can understand **why** God would want us to wait on some things. It doesn't make the wait easy. There are times when it can feel miserable and flat out dumb. Yet we know that He sets these guidelines in place for us so that when it *is* time, we can enjoy such a wonderful gift just as He has intended for us to enjoy it.

Journal:

Day 10, Season #1:

Date: _____ / _____ / _____

WHAT DO YOU THINK WILL BE A BENEFIT TO WAITING? TRY TO THINK OF BENEFIT(S) THAT ARE NOT PHYSICAL.

_____

_____

_____

_____

Day 10, Season #2:

Date: _____ / _____ / _____

WHAT DO YOU THINK WILL BE A BENEFIT TO WAITING? TRY TO THINK OF BENEFIT(S) THAT ARE NOT PHYSICAL.

_____

_____

_____

_____

Day 10, Season #3:

Date: _____ / _____ / _____

WHAT DO YOU THINK WILL BE A BENEFIT TO WAITING? TRY TO THINK OF BENEFIT(S) THAT ARE NOT PHYSICAL.

_____

_____

_____

_____

Day 10, Season #4:

Date: _____ / _____ / _____

WHAT DO YOU THINK WILL BE A BENEFIT TO WAITING? TRY TO THINK OF BENEFIT(S) THAT ARE NOT PHYSICAL.

_____

_____

_____

_____

- DAY 11 -

to the girl wondering why her message has been "seen" or "read" and is waiting on a response...

you matter.

whether he sees it. says it. knows it or not.

you matter.

maybe he'll reply.
maybe he won't.

...you still matter.
you always have.
always will.

@JAMIEGRACEH

- DAY 12 -

I love a good step-by-step process. No matter how many times I've made Chicken Parmesan, you'll always find me reading through the recipe before I start and throughout the entire process. While there is no exact step-by-step or timeline for our lives, I've found that there are three steps that can motivate toward making a positive change.

The first step is to **acknowledge** or **accept.** Ask yourself, what is it that you want to acknowledge? What is the choice that you are making?

When no one is home, or close enough to think you might be going cray, take a trip back to your bathroom. Stand in front of the mirror, look yourself in the eyes and take a deep breath. Then, finish the sentence "I am waiting to…"

Then, say it again. This time without the fear that your neighbors or roommates can hear you. Say it with a smile. Not a creepy too-much grin. But enough confidence so that you believe it. Then, add the **why.** "I am waiting to… because…" and say it like you mean it.

Say it every day if you want to.
Say it every hour if you need to.
Say it once a week if it helps.
Say it to yourself as you're swiping if you know you need it (y'all know what apps I'm talking about).

Make the **choice** to know what you're waiting for - and own it.

1) Acknowledge:

What are you waiting for?

Journal:

Day 12, Season #1:

Date: _____ / _____ / _____

What are you waiting for? What is your intention for waiting? _____

_____

_____

_____

Day 12, Season #2:

Date: _____ / _____ / _____

What are you waiting for? What is your intention for waiting? _____

_____

_____

_____

DAY 12, SEASON #3:

DATE: _____ / _____ / _____

WHAT ARE YOU WAITING FOR? WHAT IS YOUR INTENTION FOR WAITING? _____

_____

_____

_____

DAY 12, SEASON #4:

DATE: _____ / _____ / _____

WHAT ARE YOU WAITING FOR? WHAT IS YOUR INTENTION FOR WAITING? _____

_____

_____

_____

- Day 13 -

The second step is to take **action**. You have acknowledged and accepted what you're waiting for and *now* you own it. You live your life to the fullest. You're not in a no-sex-box, you're in a season of waiting. And life hasn't lost it's streak of incredible. You spend time with friends, work hard in your career, give your all to your education, pursue your dreams, invest in your family, start new hobbies, read a million books, go on cool vacations - you live life.

Simultaneously, you actively wait.

If you're going on dates or are in a relationship, you will need to set boundaries. When Aaron I were engaged, we were both able to openly say, "I need to go now," or "I need you to go home now." We had numerous conversations about our boundaries and expectations and actively held each other accountable for not crossing lines that we didn't want to cross.

You **have** to set boundaries for yourself. Maybe this means that you and your boyfriend don't spend 1-on-1 time in your bedroom. Or maybe you don't spend your 3am making out in a car listening to music that's about more than making out. **You** have to set these boundaries. *Then* you have to be honest, bold and open about them.

I've been the girl on a date awkwardly dodging a goodnight kiss followed by, "Oh by the way… that's not happening. But I had a great night!" Is it odd? Yeah man. Very much so. But it's an honest and bold representation of setting boundaries and keeping them.

Pro Tip: The date that's worth keep around will not only respect your
boundaries, but will ask that you respect theirs too.

2) Action:

Wait.

Journal:

Day 13, Season #1:

Date: _____ / _____ / _____

What are some physical and emotional boundaries that you want to set in your current or future relationship?

_____
_____
_____
_____

What are some practical ways that you can occupy your time while you wait?_____

_____
_____
_____

Day 13, Season #2:

Date: _____ / _____ / _____

WHAT ARE SOME PHYSICAL AND EMOTIONAL BOUNDARIES THAT
YOU WANT TO SET IN YOUR CURRENT OR FUTURE RELATIONSHIP?

_____

_____

_____

_____

WHAT ARE SOME PRACTICAL WAYS THAT YOU CAN OCCUPY YOUR
TIME WHILE YOU WAIT?_____

_____

_____

_____

DAY 13, SEASON #3:

DATE: _____ / _____ / _____

WHAT ARE SOME PHYSICAL AND EMOTIONAL BOUNDARIES THAT
YOU WANT TO SET IN YOUR CURRENT OR FUTURE RELATIONSHIP?

_____

_____

_____

_____

WHAT ARE SOME PRACTICAL WAYS THAT YOU CAN OCCUPY YOUR
TIME WHILE YOU WAIT?_____

_____

_____

_____

DAY 13, SEASON #4:

DATE: _____ / _____ / _____

WHAT ARE SOME PHYSICAL AND EMOTIONAL BOUNDARIES THAT
YOU WANT TO SET IN YOUR CURRENT OR FUTURE RELATIONSHIP?

_____

_____

_____

_____

WHAT ARE SOME PRACTICAL WAYS THAT YOU CAN OCCUPY YOUR
TIME WHILE YOU WAIT?_____

_____

_____

_____

- DAY 14 -

The third and final step is **accountability.** Please don't think that this awesome, challenging, exciting and sometimes awkward journey of waiting should ever be done alone! You need the wisdom, love and calling-out-ed-ness of those around you and there's nothing wrong with that.

I have a small group of women in my life that I know I can always call when needed. They not only encourage me when I ask for it, but they also call *me* when I don't even know that I need it (Or when I'm being a brat and don't want it).

When I post something on social media that may seem too dramatic or anxiety-driven - I get a call. When I reach an exciting career milestone - I get a call. And when Aaron and I were engaged - I made a lot of calls. Ha!

One of the greatest gifts one of my mentors, Rachel Hockett, could have ever given me was the reminder of God's grace through the things we don't understand. She's married, with two kids, and also waited. She told me hilariously awkward and adorable stories that happened leading up to her wedding and in the early months right after.

She helped me navigate through the insecurities of the things I didn't understand, while continually pushing me to take everything on my heart to the feet of Jesus. She laughed with me, cried with me and prayed with me. She called me out and heard me out. She wasn't on "my side" or encouraging me to be on hers. She knew what I had acknowledged, what action I was taking, and held me accountable to it.

Accountability is not
- a glorified word for a friendship.
- the cool person we know giving us advice via text or DM.
- 10 or 15 people knowing every detail and giving their input.

Accountability is intentionally seeking out the older, wiser people in our community and choosing to let them in our lives.

Accountability is answering their phone calls and listening to their wisdom even when we think we know it all. Accountability is a choice to make the call to share our brokenness and hurt, even when we know we've made a mistake. Accountability is simultaneously receiving constructive criticism so that we grow and love so that we grow properly.

Accountability takes sincere vulnerability and humility. We need the mentors, pastors and parents in our lives that don't always tell us what we want to hear but instead choose to tell us what we *need* to hear. We need to seek out people who aren't there to only listen to our problems, but to actively help us find solutions. We need people that will call us out when they see us do, say, text or even post something that is against who we are or who we want to be.

We need accountability.

3) Accountability:

Choose to reach out to two people in your life who are older and wiser than you are. Let them know what you have chosen to acknowledge, that you are taking action, and that you would love for their accountability.

If you find it increasingly difficult to find a strong mentor or accountability partner in your community, note that it may take a little work. Check out the free podcast "The Jamie Grace Podcast" (on iTunes, Spotify, etc.) for an episode all about this. Episode 110: When You Don't Want To Church-Hop But You Need Community

Bonus: as much as you can, choose to surround yourself with friends who have similar convictions and goals as yours. Your entire community shouldn't be a mirror. Yet you should build genuine friendships with men and women of a like mind, so that you can all encourage each other.

Journal:

Day 14, Season #1:

DATE: _____ / _____ / _____

WHO ARE YOU ASKING TO HOLD YOU ACCOUNTABLE?

1. _____

2. _____

WHY DID YOU CHOOSE THESE PEOPLE?

1. _____

_____

2. _____

_____

HOW WILL THEY HOLD YOU ACCOUNTABLE? (PHONE CALLS,
EMAILS, QUARTERLY COFFEE MEET-UPS, ETC.)

1. _____

2. _____

Day 14, Season #2:

DATE: _____ / _____ / _____

WHO ARE YOU ASKING TO HOLD YOU ACCOUNTABLE?

1. _____

2. _____

WHY DID YOU CHOOSE THESE PEOPLE?

1. _____

_____

2. _____

_____

HOW WILL THEY HOLD YOU ACCOUNTABLE? (PHONE CALLS,
EMAILS, QUARTERLY COFFEE MEET-UPS, ETC.)

1. _____

2. _____

DAY 14, SEASON #3:

DATE: _____ / _____ / _____

WHO ARE YOU ASKING TO HOLD YOU ACCOUNTABLE?

1. _____

2. _____

WHY DID YOU CHOOSE THESE PEOPLE?

1. _____

_____

2. _____

_____

HOW WILL THEY HOLD YOU ACCOUNTABLE? (PHONE CALLS, EMAILS, QUARTERLY COFFEE MEET-UPS, ETC.)

1. _____

2. _____

DAY 14, SEASON #4:

DATE: _____ / _____ / _____

WHO ARE YOU ASKING TO HOLD YOU ACCOUNTABLE?

1. _____

2. _____

WHY DID YOU CHOOSE THESE PEOPLE?

1. _____
_____

2. _____
_____

HOW WILL THEY HOLD YOU ACCOUNTABLE? (PHONE CALLS, EMAILS, QUARTERLY COFFEE MEET-UPS, ETC.)

1. _____

2. _____

- Day 15 -

Waiting is incredible.

It's awkward.

Sometimes challenging.

Often misunderstood.

Seldom pursued.

But waiting is incredible.

Know that while you're waiting, you're not asking God to take your desire to have sex away. You're not asking God to turn you heart away from all things intimate and romantic. You're asking him for the guidance and the will to wait until it's the right time.

DAUGHTERS OF JERUSALEM, I CHARGE YOU
BY THE GAZELLES AND BY THE DOES OF THE FIELD:
DO NOT AROUSE OR AWAKEN LOVE
UNTIL IT SO DESIRES.
-SONG OF SOLOMON 2:7

You have made a decision to wait. You're gonna have days where you watch more romantic comedies and listen to more sappy love songs that you know you need to. But you'll also have days where you get right back up, with an exceptional amount of confidence, and start a new day.

If you allow it, the good in the waiting will **far** outweigh the bad. If you allow it, you will live a life of joy, hope, love and freedom while you wait. If you allow it, you will become more and more dependent on The Source, which will naturally allow you to become more and more confident in your choices. You will understand that marriage isn't a reward and singlehood isn't a curse. You're simply in this season right here, right now - and it's a beautiful thing.

It's beautiful to desire love. It's admirable to want to be told that you're beautiful, funny, fun to be around and downright gorgeous or handsome. If you find yourself becoming anxious or frustrated because you long for attention or a physical connection - there's nothing wrong with you. You simply have a desire to be seen, heard and cared about.

By desiring to be loved, you are acknowledging that you deserve to be loved. And the best part of all, is that you already are.

I love my husband. Real talk. He's my best friend and even though we haven't even been married for a year, I can't imagine my life without him. But as great as he is, when I wake up every morning, my first role is not wife.

My first title, every morning, is daughter of the King. No matter how long I'm married and get to be a wife (mutual plan is forever), no matter how many kids we have someday running around calling me "mom," I will always be a daughter of the King **first.**

When I choose to find my worth and my value in being a wife, friend, daughter, aunt or even mom, my joy is contingent on those things. My hope only thrives when my marriage, friendships and family life are smooth sailing. But what if my husband isn't feeling joyful one day? What if the rest of my family or all of my friends aren't feeling hopeful? The second one of those things has a less than perfect moment - my hope, my joy and my strength begin to decrease.

However, when I choose to find my worth and value in being a daughter of the King, I am investing all of who I am into a perfect Source whose love is inevitable. He never has a less than perfect moment and will continually provide hope, joy and strength.

Whether single, dating, engaged or married, we have to embrace our first title. The most important title. We need to celebrate who we are at the core of our identity so that we know that every desire we have to be loved, seen, cherished and heard has already been met and will never end.

DAY 15, SEASON #1:

DATE: _____ / _____ / _____

WHAT IS YOUR FIRST TITLE? _____
_____

HOW DOES EMBRACING YOUR FIRST TITLE HAVE AN IMPACT ON
YOUR DECISION TO WAIT? _____
_____
_____
_____

ARE YOU PROUD OF YOUR DECISION TO WAIT? _____

WHAT WOULD YOU SAY TO ENCOURAGE YOURSELF ON THE DAYS
WHEN WAITING IS HARDER THAN OTHERS? _____
_____
_____
_____
_____
_____
_____
_____
_____

DAY 15, SEASON #2:

DATE: _____ / _____ / _____

WHAT IS YOUR FIRST TITLE? _____
_____

HOW DOES EMBRACING YOUR FIRST TITLE HAVE AN IMPACT ON
YOUR DECISION TO WAIT? _____
_____
_____
_____

ARE YOU PROUD OF YOUR DECISION TO WAIT? _____

WHAT WOULD YOU SAY TO ENCOURAGE YOURSELF ON THE DAYS
WHEN WAITING IS HARDER THAN OTHERS? _____
_____
_____
_____
_____
_____
_____
_____
_____

Day 15, Season #3:

Date: _____ / _____ / _____

What is your first title? _____

_____

How does embracing your first title have an impact on your decision to wait? _____

_____

_____

_____

Are you proud of your decision to wait? _____

What would you say to encourage yourself on the days when waiting is harder than others? _____

_____

_____

_____

_____

_____

_____

_____

DAY 15, SEASON #4:

DATE: _____ / _____ / _____

WHAT IS YOUR FIRST TITLE? _____

_____

HOW DOES EMBRACING YOUR FIRST TITLE HAVE AN IMPACT ON
YOUR DECISION TO WAIT? _____

_____

_____

_____

ARE YOU PROUD OF YOUR DECISION TO WAIT? _____

WHAT WOULD YOU SAY TO ENCOURAGE YOURSELF ON THE DAYS
WHEN WAITING IS HARDER THAN OTHERS? _____

_____

_____

_____

_____

_____

_____

_____

_____

- Final Thoughts -

I wanted to wait until I was married to actually say this because I didn't want to offend anyone. So here goes: Y'all, **married people can stress me out sometimes**.

When I was single (for my literal entire life until November 2017), I was constantly asked when I was going to settle down. There were married people who thought that I traveled / toured / worked too much and as a Christian woman in my 20s I should be at home, with my children, and certainly nowhere near a tour bus.

When I mentioned that I couldn't *wait* to be a wife, a mom and prayerfully even a homeschool mom of all 5+ of my children, the immediate response was that that was way too many children, I was "doing too much" and I needed to wait on the man that God had for me. Then I would typically hear something like, "It'll happen when you least expect it" or "Trust me, you've got time. I didn't meet my husband until I was 83."

There was a constant battle of extremes. My singlehood no longer felt like a season to enjoy but instead a platform that constantly welcomed opinions and advice that often contradicted themselves if I stayed in the conversation long enough. I was overwhelmed, frustrated and tempted to allow the grand finale to be consistent isolation.

I got married in April 2018. Aaron Collins is my best friend, the love of my life and our life together has been full of more joy and hope than I could have ever anticipated. Leading up to our wedding day, I *did* face fears and worries - but none of them had to do with us. I was **so afraid** of becoming **that** married lady with a pocket full of advice full of pride and lacking grace. While wisdom is shouting and we shouldn't ever turn away, I worried that in my efforts to encourage others I would sound like the same broken records that nearly broke me years before.

The best thing that I could do to not talk myself out of writing songs and books about dating and relationships, was to focus on the **good** that carried me through my season of singlehood. For every unfortunate conversation and awkward commentary on my love life (or complete lack thereof), God showed up in ways that only He can.

I was surrounded by couples, singles and families who encouraged me, called me out, loved on me, supported me and *most* of all led beautiful lives that set incredible examples for me.

At an early age, I **acknowledged** that I wanted to wait.

I set boundaries for every date that I went on and my fiancé (now husband) and I certainly took **action** in setting boundaries and revisiting those conversations as often as we needed to.

Throughout my singlehood, our courtship and engagement, I intentionally surrounded myself with older, wiser women who I could not only call at any time but would call *me* out at *all* times to hold me **accountable** to being the woman that I was and wanted to be.

Even in marriage, those three steps play a significant role in my life. Whether you're waiting for a job, an acceptance letter for a college, the moment you become a parent - we'll *always* be learning, growing - and **waiting**.

The goal is to be able to embrace the beauty of every moment and every season exactly as God has given them to us. Because no matter what the outcome, I can promise you that it will be worth the wait.